Contents

T0025881

Introduction

F ruits, vegetables, grains, meat, and dairy can all be part of a healthy diet, but there is often more to these foods than can be seen on the surface. They contain nutrients and proteins that keep your body strong and help you grow. However, many items in a grocery store also have extra chemicals that are used during the process of growing or raising the food. These chemicals include antibiotics, pesticides, and hormones.

Antibiotics are strong medicines that are used to cure diseases. They can keep food-producing animals healthy when used correctly. Pesticides are chemicals that are applied to crops in order to keep pests like insects, weeds, and rodents from destroying food. Hormones are chemical messengers that are naturally produced by human and animal bodies. When extra natural or **synthetic** hormones are given to dairy- and meat-producing animals, they can increase their growth or production of food.

Antibiotics, pesticides, and hormones have many benefits for producing large quantities of food, protecting animals and crops from diseases and pests, and preventing food waste. They were developed as tools to increase and protect the food supply.

Three government agencies oversee the use of antibiotics, pesticides, and hormones in the United States. The Food and Drug Administration (FDA) regulates the use of antibiotics and hormones. The Environmental Protection Agency (EPA), the U.S. Department of Agriculture (USDA), and the FDA all have roles to play in managing pesticides.

Be Smart About

Antibiotics, Pesticides, and Hormones

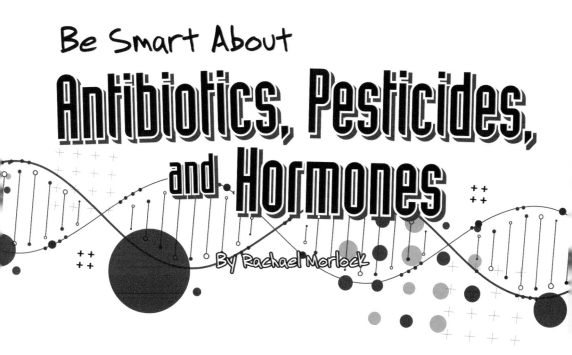

By Rachael Morlock

Cavendish Square

Published in 2023 by Cavendish Square Publishing, LLC
2544 Clinton Street, Buffalo, NY 14224

Website: cavendishsq.com

This publication represents the opinions and views of the author based on his or her personal experience, knowledge, and research. The information in this book serves as a general guide only. The author and publisher have used their best efforts in preparing this book and disclaim liability rising directly or indirectly from the use and application of this book.

Disclaimer: Portions of this work were originally authored by Katharina Smundak and published as *The Truth Behind Antibiotics, Pesticides, and Hormones* (From Factory to Table: What You're Really Eating). All new material this edition authored by Rachael Morlock.

All websites were available and accurate when this book was sent to press.

Library of Congress Cataloging-in-Publication Data

Names: Morlock, Rachael, author.
Title: Be smart about antibiotics, pesticides, and hormones / Rachael Morlock.
Description: Buffalo, New York : Cavendish Square Publishing, [2023] | Series: The truth about your food | Includes index.
Identifiers: LCCN 2022027872 | ISBN 9781502665911 (library binding) | ISBN 9781502665904 (paperback) | ISBN 9781502665928 (ebook)
Subjects: LCSH: Food–Toxicology–Juvenile literature. | Feed additives–Juvenile literature. | Antibiotics in animal nutrition–Juvenile literature. | Hormones in animal nutrition–Juvenile literature. | Pesticide residues in feed–Juvenile literature. | Pesticide residues in food–Juvenile literature.
Classification: LCC RA1258 .M64 2023 | DDC 615.9/54–dc23/eng/20220628
LC record available at https://lccn.loc.gov/2022027872

Editor: Rachael Morlock
Copyeditor: Shannon Harts
Designer: Deanna Paternostro

The photographs in this book are used by permission and through the courtesy of: Cover (main), p. 11 Fotokostic/Shutterstock.com; cover (DNA graphic), back cover, pp. 3, 4, 7, 14, 17, 24, 27, 28, 33, 38-39, 42-43, 44-45, 46-47, 48 Omelchenko/Shutterstock.com; p. 5 8th.creator/Shutterstock.com; p. 6 Anna Hoychuk/Shutterstock.com; p. 8 Kallayanee Naloka/Shutterstock.com; p. 13 Ratthaphong Ekariyasap/Shutterstock.com; p. 14 Halibutt/Wikimedia Commons; p. 16 NaMong Productions/Shutterstock.com; pp. 18-19 pobpra story/Shutterstock.com; p. 20 Rhys Leonard/Shutterstock.com; p. 22 Designua/Shutterstock.com; p. 26 Marina Rose/Shutterstock.com; p. 28 Animalparty/Wikimedia Commons; p. 30 Hakim Graphy/Shutterstock.com; p. 31 Clark Ukidu/Shutterstock.com; p. 32 RozenskiP/Shutterstock.com; p. 36 Tada Images/Shutterstock.com; p. 37 Catherine Eckert/Shutterstock.com; p. 39 BearFotos/Shutterstock.com; p. 40 Romiana Lee/Shutterstock.com.

Some of the images in this book illustrate individuals who are models. The depictions do not imply actual situations or events.

CPSIA compliance information: Batch #CW23CSQ: For further information, contact Cavendish Square Publishing LLC at 1-877-980-4450.

Printed in the United States of America

Find us on

> Eating fruits and vegetables is one of the most powerful things you can do for your body. It's more important to eat a variety of fruits and vegetables than it is to avoid all pesticides.

These agencies have determined that some antibiotics, pesticides, and hormones are safe to use to produce food. However, many people worry about their effects on the environment and in our bodies. For that reason, most foods are labeled to let buyers know if they have been made with or without these products.

A certified organic label from the USDA is the easiest way to tell if a food has been produced without hormones and antibiotics and with limited, if any, pesticides. The USDA has strict rules for how certified organic foods are raised and produced. Buying food locally at a farmers market or farm store gives you the opportunity to ask questions about how food is grown or how animals are raised.

Antibiotics, pesticides, and hormones can have both positive and negative effects now and in the future. Learning what it means to use antibiotics, pesticides, and hormones in food production can influence your decisions about the foods you want to eat.

An assortment of fruits, vegetables, grains, and proteins are part of a healthy diet, but even healthy foods can contain unhealthy substances depending on how they're produced.

Chapter One

Tools for Food Production

In modern farming, antibiotics, pesticides, and hormones have been used to create a more productive food system. The growing world population is one factor in the push to produce more food using limited resources. Each year, the world population increases by about 83 million people, and the total population is expected to climb to 9.8 billion by 2050. This will create a much greater demand for food, and farmers must meet the challenge using the best tools available. However, feeding a growing world means not only producing more food but also using it well. For example, food waste is a problem in the United States, where 40 percent of the food that is grown and produced is never eaten. Food should also be produced with as little harm to people, animals, and the environment as possible. Antibiotics, pesticides, and hormones are tools for producing more food, but they also have disadvantages.

Antibiotics and Bacteria

Most people are familiar with antibiotics as the medication they take when they're sick. The discovery of antibiotics has

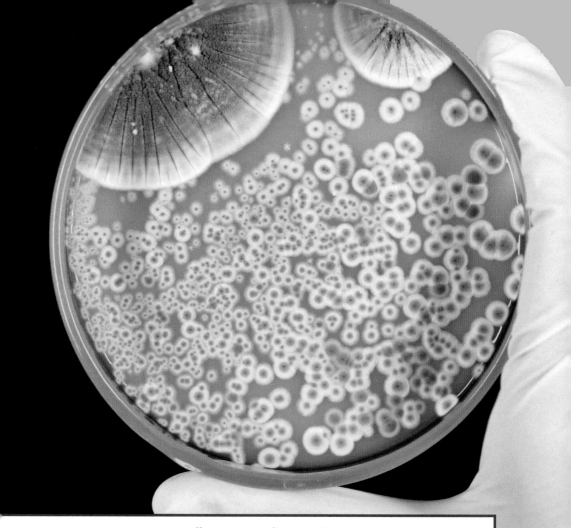

The antibiotic penicillin is developed from a type of mold called *Penicillium*, shown here being grown in a lab.

saved millions and millions of lives because these medicines kill bacteria. Antibiotics are produced from bacteria, molds, and other fungi.

In September 1928, Sir Alexander Fleming, a professor at St. Mary's Hospital in London, England, went on vacation. When he came back, he inspected the petri dishes on which he had started growing *Staphylococcus* bacteria. Bacterial colonies dotted his petri dishes, but he noticed something strange about one of them: A mold had **contaminated** it, and no colonies grew directly around it. This mold was *Penicillium*, and it prevented bacteria from growing. It was then used to make the antibiotic penicillin.

From there, a scientist named Howard Florey and others working at Oxford University started developing methods to make penicillin available on a large scale. The medicine saved many lives during World War II (1939–1945) by preventing soldiers from dying of infections like bacterial pneumonia.

Just like humans, animals can get bacterial infections. This is one reason farmers give them antibiotics. Beginning in the 1940s, farmers used growth-promoting antibiotics (GPAs) to make animals gain weight faster. Then, these animals required less food to gain weight. GPAs were given to animals in small amounts, which meant the dose was not high enough to kill all the bacteria. As a result, bacteria not killed by the antibiotics reproduced and passed on their **resistance** to future generations.

Antibiotic-resistant bacteria is so dangerous that the FDA restricted the use of GPAs by law in 2017. The law resulted in a ban on 80 different GPAs for food-producing animals. Now farmers are only permitted to give animals antibiotics to treat or prevent infections and not to promote growth, and they must be used with the guidance of a veterinarian.

According to the Centers for Disease Control and Prevention (CDC), antibiotic-resistant bacteria can enter our food supply in different ways. One way is when the bacteria contaminate the meat of slaughtered animals. Another is when animal waste containing resistant bacteria gets into the environment. It can be used in fertilizer or enter water that is later used on crops. These bacteria can remain on the fruits and vegetables that people eat at home.

When people become infected with antibiotic-resistant bacteria, doctors need to prescribe more and stronger antibiotics to kill the bacteria. At some point, bacteria may develop resistance to all known antibiotics, and humans may no longer have antibiotics strong enough to fight the bacteria. Antibiotic resistance is a major public health problem.

Pesticides and Residues

Pesticides can also be harmful to humans. Pesticides are substances that prevent, repel, or destroy pests, which can come in the form of insects, weeds, fungi, or rodents. Pesticides can be insecticides, herbicides, fungicides, or rodenticides. They are used in gardens and in homes, but they are also applied on a massive scale to crops. About 1 billion pounds (453 billion kilograms) of pesticides are used in the United States each year.

Pesticides enter the food chain in multiple ways. The first way is direct: They are applied to the crops that humans eat. Small amounts of pesticides can remain on or in these foods as **residues**. Because pesticides are sprayed, wind can also carry them through the air into rivers or other farms. Furthermore, they can seep through the soil and enter groundwater. They can also remain on the surface of the ground and enter our water supply as part of surface runoff, which is the flow of water over land.

For humans, pesticides are dangerous because they can act as endocrine disruptors (EDs). These are chemicals our bodies respond to like hormones. They are very likely to be carcinogenic, or able to cause cancer, in humans. According to the EPA, EDs not only increase the risk of cancer, but they also interfere with reproduction, disturb **nervous system** and **immune system** function, and affect development. There is evidence that people who are consistently exposed to pesticides, such as people who spray crops, have higher rates of certain cancers as well as problems with their nervous systems, livers, and motor function (which is their ability to control how their body moves).

In industrial agriculture, or the large-scale production of crops for food, pesticides are sprayed on crops.

Hormones and Development

Hormones are another substance sometimes given to animals to promote growth. They are chemical messengers that regulate various reactions in the body. In humans, they play an important role in reproduction, growth, and energy regulation. Two types of hormones are steroids and proteins.

In the United States, steroids are given to cattle and sheep in order to make them grow faster and transform the food they're eating into fat and muscle more efficiently. These hormones are only given to beef cattle and sheep, not to dairy cows, veal calves, pigs, or poultry. Steroids in pellet form are attached surgically to the back of cattle ears. This implant slowly dissolves over the course of the animal's life as the steroids enter the bloodstream. The ears are then discarded, or thrown away, once the animal is slaughtered.

Cattle used for meat can be treated with six hormones, three of which are natural estrogen, progesterone, and testosterone. The other three are synthetic versions of these same hormones. All six hormones are banned for this use in the European Union (EU). Indeed, hormone-treated beef is illegal in the EU and is not allowed for import. In 1999, the EU's Scientific Committee on Veterinary Measures Relating to Public Health published a report that concluded that hormones used for meat had potentially negative hormonal and developmental effects for humans.

A growth hormone called recombinant bovine growth hormone (rBGH) is given to dairy cows to increase their milk production. It is also called recombinant bovine somatotropin (rBST). The FDA approved rBGH in 1993, but it is banned in the EU, Canada, Japan, Australia, and New Zealand. Some countries have banned rBGH over concerns for animal health and welfare. In the United States, rBGH use has been declining since many shoppers look for products made without it.

Hormones are not currently approved for use in chickens in the United States. So when chicken is labeled "hormone-free" at the supermarket, it's true. Technically, it's been true for all chickens for decades.

Like antibiotic-resistant bacteria, animal hormones can end up in our bodies both through the food we eat or through animal waste, which often enters our water supply. Synthetic hormones are endocrine disruptors, just like pesticides.

In the end, the danger of hormones depends on the quantities in which they're consumed. In a child who hasn't yet gone through **puberty**, these small quantities of hormones could have stronger effects than on an adult. The hormone levels in the meat we eat are a fraction of the hormone levels we produce ourselves, so whether or not hormone-treated meat is bad for humans is a subject of debate and further research.

Some dairy cows are given rBGH to make them produce more milk, which can be collected by milking machines.

Using rBGH to increase milk production in cows raises two important issues. The first is whether or not the hormone can directly affect humans. Since it is not a human hormone, any rBGH that remains in milk is broken down in your stomach and is not active in your body. However, the milk of cows treated with rBGH also contains higher levels of a hormone called insulin-like growth factor, or IGF-1. Having high levels of this hormone has been connected with the development of breast, prostate, colorectal, and other cancers. More research is needed to determine if drinking milk from rBGH-treated cows puts you at greater risk for developing cancer.

The second issue of using rBGH has to do with increased antibiotic use in dairy cows. Cows that produce more milk as a result of rBGH are more likely to get mastitis—an infection of the cow's udders that is generally treated with antibiotics. This increases the risk that antibiotic-resistant bacteria will develop and spread. Overall, rBGH has been found to have harmful health effects for animals, but the extent to which it affects human health is still unknown.

The milk from a cow with mastitis cannot be used for a certain period of time to make sure there's no trace of antibiotics.

Timeline of Bovine Growth Hormone

1930s: Farmers inject cows with bovine growth hormone (bGH) for the first time.

1980s: Scientists develop a new version of bGH using DNA technology and name it rBGH.

1990: A group of European countries bans the use of rBGH in dairy cows.

1993: The FDA approves the use of rBGH in dairy cows.

1999: Canada bans the use of rBGH in dairy cows.

2000: The EU officially bans rBGH.

2003: The FDA determines that milk products with the extra growth hormones do not require special labels.

> Since the 1930s, when bovine growth hormone was discovered to increase milk production, new technologies and new restrictions have changed the way the hormone is used in dairy cows.

Food for Thought

1. Why should or shouldn't foods produced with antibiotics, hormones, or pesticides be labeled?
2. Are there times when it's necessary to give food-producing animals antibiotics?
3. Do you think the United States needs to use pesticides and hormones to produce enough food? Why or why not?

Washing and then peeling fruits and vegetables makes them safer to eat, especially if they've come in contact with pesticides or bacteria. Firm fruits and vegetables can also be scrubbed.

Chapter Two

Effects on Health

One of the major concerns with antibiotics, pesticides, and hormones is that they are unhealthy for humans. Antibiotics provide a perfect example of how a tool for increasing food production can also have negative consequences. Using antibiotics to keep animals healthy might benefit them in the short term, but in the long term it can be very dangerous for both humans and animals as antibiotic-resistant bacteria develop and increase.

Antibiotics are used, and often overused, to treat and prevent illnesses on farms. In fact, about 65 percent of the antibiotics in the United States are given to food-producing animals. Only 35 percent are used as medicines for humans.

The overuse of antibiotics has very real consequences for people today. According to the CDC, about 2.8 million antibiotic-resistant infections occur every year in the United States. These infections result in more than 35,000 deaths. Antibiotic-resistant infections can affect anyone, regardless of age or health.

Dangerous Bacteria

Each year, about 48 million people become sick with illnesses carried by food. The infection-causing bacteria in food that present the greatest threat to humans are *Escherichia coli* (most commonly known as *E. coli*), *Salmonella*, and *Campylobacter*.

Some *E. coli* strains are present in our lower intestines, and they cause no harm at all. Other strains result in foodborne illnesses. Normally, eating food contaminated with *E. coli* causes mild food poisoning, but it can also have more serious consequences. It can be avoided by washing produce properly, keeping meat separate from other foods, and cooking meat to the correct temperature.

Salmonella is another bacterium that can cause food poisoning. As with *E. coli*, humans can be infected with *Salmonella* by eating improperly cooked meat. It can also be found in raw eggs, raw milk, and on produce washed with water that contains the bacteria.

The symptoms of *Salmonella* poisoning are fever, stomach cramps, and diarrhea, which can lead to dehydration. For healthy adults, *Salmonella* poisoning is not life-threatening. However, it is dangerous and even deadly for older adults, children, babies, pregnant women, and people with other health problems.

It's important to prepare meat on a separate cutting board so that bacteria from the meat doesn't contaminate foods that will be eaten raw.

Pets and farm animals can pass on dangerous bacteria even when they're healthy. Be sure to wash your hands after handling animals and before eating.

Not all antibiotic-resistant bacteria is carried by food. An outbreak of *Salmonella* Heidelberg in 2016 in the United States spread directly between farm animals and people. Calves infected with this antibiotic-resistant strain of *Salmonella* passed the bacterium on to children and farmers who came in contact with them. The outbreak occurred across multiple states, and the *Salmonella* was resistant to multiple kinds of antibiotics.

Eating food contaminated with *Campylobacter* leads to campylobacteriosis. The symptoms are similar to *Salmonella* poisoning: diarrhea, fever, and stomach cramps. Campylobacteriosis comes from eating undercooked, contaminated chicken. Other meats, such as pork, or contaminated milk and water can also cause an infection. Most of the time, no treatment is required, but for people with weak immune systems, the infection can be very serious and require antibiotic treatment. The use of antibiotics in food-producing animals has also resulted in antibiotic-resistant *Campylobacter*.

Endocrine Disruptors

Some synthetic hormones and pesticides disrupt, or interfere with, the endocrine system in various ways. The endocrine system is a collection of glands that secrete hormones. Even small changes in the way the endocrine system functions can affect growth, development, and reproduction in humans and animals.

The body responds to endocrine disruptors as if they were natural hormones. Some endocrine disruptors block hormone receptors. Others lead to the overproduction or underproduction of hormones.

Endocrine System

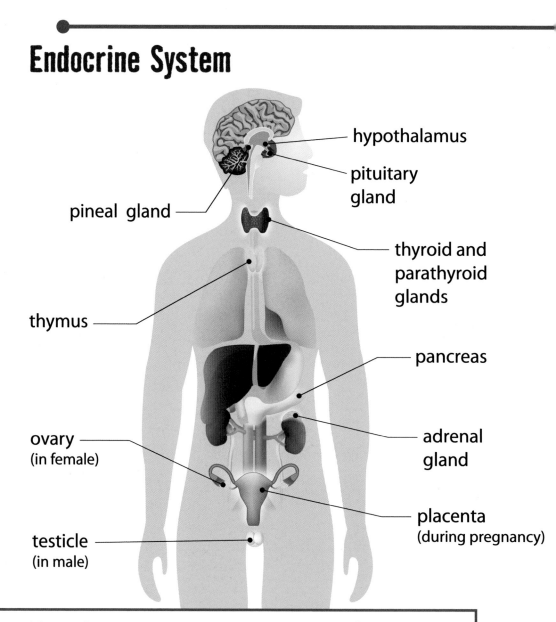

hypothalamus

pituitary gland

pineal gland

thyroid and parathyroid glands

thymus

pancreas

ovary
(in female)

adrenal gland

testicle
(in male)

placenta
(during pregnancy)

The endocrine system is made up of many glands throughout the body, as shown in this diagram. These glands produce hormones that control and coordinate different processes, such as metabolism, growth, development, and reproduction.

Endocrine disruptors can play a big role during important and sensitive stages in the life cycle like pregnancy and childhood development. Endocrine disruptors are also considered a reason for widespread cases of puberty starting earlier than normal.

Some hormones and pesticides have been banned because of the negative effects they have on human health. In the 1930s, scientists developed diethylstilbestrol (DES), a synthetic estrogen. This hormone was used beginning in the 1950s to increase growth in cattle and chickens. From 1940 to 1971, it was prescribed to pregnant women to prevent miscarriages, or the loss of pregnancy. By the late 1960s, doctors noticed that women whose mothers had taken DES while pregnant with them were more likely to have a certain kind of cancer. DES was also found to cause health problems, such as **sterility**, in the farm workers who gave it to cattle and chickens. In 1971, the FDA banned the use of DES in humans and in farm animals. It is now considered an endocrine disruptor.

Health and Pesticides

Pesticides are very dangerous for people who come in close contact with large amounts of them. Farm workers and people who live near agricultural fields are most at risk. This type of exposure to pesticides has been linked to multiple diseases and health conditions, such as asthma, **Parkinson's disease**, **Alzheimer's disease**, reproductive problems, type 2 diabetes, and various cancers.

In 2015, the International Agency for Research on Cancer determined that three common pesticides are probably

Pesticides in Food

Most people are exposed to pesticides through the food they eat and the water they drink. The EPA decides what amount of pesticides should be allowed to remain on food. The FDA and the USDA perform tests on food to make sure that only these small amounts are present as residues.

Even though the government has determined that small amounts are safe, pesticides may still be harmful to health over time. In addition, the effects of consuming many different kinds of pesticides together are unknown.

Children are most at risk for problems due to exposure to pesticides because they are going through important stages of development. A study found that children ages 8 to 15 with high levels of a chemical in their urine that shows exposure to pyrethroid pesticides were more likely to have **attention-deficit/hyperactivity disorder** (ADHD). This supports the theory that exposure to pesticides can impact the way children think, learn, and behave.

carcinogens. Glyphosate is one of these pesticides, and it's one of the most widely used pesticides in the United States. Its use is important for **genetically engineered** (GE) crops, but it is linked with a type of cancer called non-Hodgkin's lymphoma.

Although the EPA determines which pesticides can be used and has banned some toxic substances, the United States uses many pesticides that are banned by other countries and considered harmful by the World Health Organization (WHO). In 2017, the United States used 150 pesticides that the WHO classifies as dangerous to human health. In 2019, the EPA allowed the use of 85 pesticides that are banned or being phased out in the EU, Brazil, or China.

Food for Thought

1. How do you practice food safety when preparing food at home?
2. Is it important to you to know if your food was grown with pesticides? Why or why not?
3. Why do you think the United States uses pesticides and hormones that many other countries have banned?

Foods like almonds, cherries, blueberries, and pears grow with the help of insects like bees, but pesticides put these pollinators in danger.

Chapter Three

Effects on the Environment

Antibiotic-resistant bacteria, endocrine-disrupting hormones, and pesticides have indirect impacts on humans through their effects on the environment. Using a lot of antibiotics can lead to the growth of harmful bacteria. Pesticides affect crops, but they can also affect entire ecosystems when they enter soil and water or travel in the wind. Hormones can remain in the meat or dairy that's produced and also be passed into the environment. These substances build up in animals, pollute water and soil, harm pollinators, and throw ecosystems out of balance.

Persistent Pesticides and Hormones

Pesticides and synthetic hormones pose a threat because they don't always go away after they've served their purpose in agriculture. Bioaccumulation is the way a substance builds up in an organism over time. It occurs when more of a substance remains in the body than the body gets rid of. Many pesticides are bioaccumulative because they remain in animal bodies and the environment. These substances are called persistent, bioaccumulative, and toxic (PBT) or persistent organic pollutants (POPs).

The Case of DDT

The case of dichloro-diphenyl-trychloroethane (DDT) is a good example of a POP. DDT was the first modern pesticide, developed in the 1940s. It was and continues to be used to fight the diseases typhus and malaria. In the past, it was also used as an agricultural insecticide. However, increased insect resistance to DDT meant that the insecticide became less effective over time. In addition, the environmentalist Rachel Carson wrote a book called *Silent Spring* that drew attention to the effects of DDT on the environment and birds. These factors resulted in a ban on DDT as an insecticide in 1972.

Despite the fact that DDT has been banned for more than 50 years, it is still a threat because it is a POP. Certain types of fish caught in Washington, for example, still contain DDT. Pregnant women and breastfeeding women are warned against eating such fish, as DDT can be passed from mother to child through breast milk. DDT exposure can cause mental problems, and the EPA lists it as a possible carcinogen. The FDA warns that fish grown on fish farms are also vulnerable to pesticide bioaccumulation since the food they eat may have these substances in their fatty tissues, where POPs are generally stored.

Rachel Carson (1907-1964) published her book Silent Spring in 1962.

POPs are particularly dangerous because they move up the food chain. When a creature low on the food chain, such as a clam, consumes a POP, it does not stay just in that clam. If a fish eats that clam, the POP will become concentrated in the fish. The higher up an animal is on the food chain, the greater the concentration of the POP in that animal. This is called **biomagnification**. Because we are at the top of the food chain as humans, we end up eating high concentrations of POPs.

Protecting Pollinators

The use of pesticides is linked to declines in bee, butterfly, and other pollinator populations. Bees in particular play an important part in our food supply. As pollinators, bees are the means by which certain plants reproduce. Bees take pollen from the male part of a plant and apply it to the female part of another plant. That plant can then produce a seed. This seed becomes the next generation of the plant. Crops rely on pollination to reproduce. According to the United Nations Food and Agriculture Organization, bees pollinate 71 of the 100 crops that provide 90 percent of food for humans!

As bee populations decline, scientists are searching for the cause of this very serious problem. A certain class of insecticides known as neonicotinoids has been linked to bee colony decline and death. Neonicotinoids are used in agriculture, but they're also applied to golf courses, gardens, and lawns. They are the most common type of insecticide in the United States. These insecticides are deadly, and not just to unwanted insects. They also kill or harm bees, butterflies, birds, and other wildlife.

Neonicotinoids soak into the ground and affect the plants that grow there for years by making all parts of the plant toxic. They also seep into water. A 2015 study by the U.S. Geological Survey found that more than half of the streams it sampled contained neonicotinoids. In 2018, the EU expanded a ban on certain

Beekeepers in the United States lost about 45 percent of their honeybee colonies from April 2020 to April 2021.

neonicotinoids to protect bees. Other factors that contribute to bee decline include parasites, disease, poor nutrition, and climate change.

Insecticides are designed to kill insects, so it's no surprise that they have an effect on bees. However, insecticides that wipe out bees and pollinators will only make growing food harder in the long run. We may lose some fruits and vegetables entirely if bees continue to decline.

Earthworms and Soil Health

Pesticides also affect earthworms. Earthworms play an essential role in soil health. Soil health is important for plant growth and productivity. Earthworms eat dead organisms and plant matter. They then excrete them as **cast**, which contains nitrogen and phosphate—key nutrients to help plants grow. Basically, earthworms create fertilizer for plants. Earthworms also build air pockets in soil, which make it easier for water to reach a plant's roots and create space for roots to grow more easily.

Worms are also an important part of the food chain, meaning that, like fish, their exposure to pesticides affects the animals that eat them.

Pesticides harm earthworms by lowering their reproduction rates and decreasing their size. A 2020 study showed there are fewer earthworms in soil treated with pesticides. Insecticides are especially toxic to earthworms and can impair their ability to improve soil conditions.

Pesticides play a huge role in agriculture. They kill organisms—such as mites, insects, and weeds—that are hurting the plants farmers want to grow, but they also kill helpful organisms like bees and earthworms. Farmers and governments must weigh the benefits and disadvantages of the techniques they use. Does the benefit of killing the pest and increasing crop yields outweigh the damage done to the ecosystem and risks to the humans who consume these foods?

Food for Thought

1. Do you think there is a safe amount of pesticides to use?
2. Who should decide if the benefits of killing pests outweigh the damage done to the ecosystem?
3. What can individuals do to protect pollinators?

The USDA organic logo on food provides information about how the food was produced.

Chapter Four

Finding a Balance

Trying to eat healthy foods may seem harder than ever once you know how antibiotics, pesticides, and hormones can impact your health and the environment. Fortunately, there are simple steps you can take to make the most of the extra food production these tools allow while also protecting your health.

Choosing and Preparing Food

Since pesticides and synthetic hormones have been linked to cancer and reproductive and developmental problems, it's smart to avoid them as much as possible. Make sure to wash and scrub your fruits and vegetables before eating them in order to remove pesticide residue and bacteria. Even organic produce may have pesticides that have landed on them from another field, or they may have bacteria. Peeling, when possible, is also a good way to lower the risks of consuming these substances, although you can miss out on important nutrients in the skin. Removing the outer leaves of green vegetables, such as lettuce, is another way to avoid pesticides and bacteria.

The Environmental Working Group (EWG) publishes a yearly "Shopper's Guide to Pesticides in Produce." The EWG report reflects the amount of pesticide residues in non-organic produce. It lists the 12 fruits and vegetables that, when tested, had the most pesticides on them after having been washed and peeled. This list is called "The Dirty Dozen," and strawberries are usually at the top of the list. Another EWG resource is "The Clean 15," which lists the 15 foods with the lowest pesticide residues. You can use these lists to help your family choose what produce to buy. Try to buy organic when eating foods from the dirty dozen list. You don't need to worry about pesticides as much with the Clean 15, so non-organic options are typically fine.

The Dirty Dozen

strawberries
spinach
kale, collard, and mustard greens
nectarines
apples
grapes
bell and hot peppers
cherries
peaches
pears
celery
tomatoes

The Clean 15

avocados
sweet corn
pineapple
onions
papaya
sweet peas (frozen)
asparagus
honeydew melon
kiwi
cabbage
mushrooms
cantaloupe
mangoes
watermelon
sweet potatoes

According to the EWG's 2022 Shopper's Guide to Pesticides in Produce, the "Dirty Dozen" non-organic fruits and vegetables have the highest amounts of pesticide residue, and the "Clean 15" have the lowest amounts.

When it comes to meat and fish, pesticides are often stored in the fat. Removing the fat before cooking can lower the amount of pesticides present. Also think about where the meat is from. If shoppers want to make sure the fish they buy and eat is free from harmful chemicals, they can use the Seafood Watch guide online.

Going Organic

Choosing organic foods seems like an easy solution if you want to avoid pesticides, antibiotic-resistant bacteria, and hormones. Although organic farmers use different methods than other food producers, you can't always avoid harmful substances entirely.

For example, organic farmers sometimes use pesticides. Instead of synthetic pesticides, they use natural substances. These pesticides are not necessarily safe just because they come from natural sources. Two of the most common natural pesticides, copper sulfate and rotenone, degrade slowly. Copper sulfate is also very toxic for birds and earthworms.

Still, most organic foods contain fewer pesticides than non-organic foods. Organic farmers use a variety of tools and techniques to control pests without chemical sprays. Pesticides are sometimes used, but only as a last resort when other pest management tools have failed. The extra work that goes into producing foods with organic methods means that organic foods are generally more expensive in the grocery store.

Artificial hormones can be avoided by eating certified organic or hormone-free meat, and you can look for hormone-free dairy products. If meat or dairy is bought from a local farmer, you can just ask if artificial hormones are used.

As for antibiotic-resistant bacteria, that's something you need to be careful about even with organic food. Dangerous

NO GMO INGREDIENTS® ™

SEE VERIFIED THE NESTLÉ PROCESS FOR MANUFACTURING THIS PRODUCT WITH NO GMO INGREDIENTS sgs.com/no-gmo

11g PROTEIN PER SERVING

NO rBST CHEESE

Cheese made with milk from cows not treated with rBST.†

NET WT 20 OZ (1 LB 4 OZ) 567g

If you want to avoid dairy products from cows treated with hormones, look for labels that tell you a product is free from rBST or rBGH.

bacteria can spread to organic vegetables through water and soil, so they should be washed and scrubbed just like non-organic produce. Organic meat also needs to be cooked properly to be sure that any bacteria is killed.

Room for Improvement

Since pesticide use can be a problem, new techniques are being adopted to lower their use. Integrated pest management (IPM) is a method for managing and controlling pests. Getting rid of entire pest populations is unlikely and impossible. Instead, IPM focuses on establishing acceptable levels of a pest, observing crops, using natural controls—such as insects that are predators for specific pests, or beneficial fungi—and, finally, only using pesticides when necessary, not as the first choice for pest management.

An important part of integrated pest management is identifying which pests are affecting crops in order to come up with effective solutions.

Safe Meat

The CDC provides helpful guidelines for preparing and cooking meat to avoid antibiotic-resistant bacteria on your food. These guidelines are broken down into four separate phases: clean, separate, cook, and chill.

Keep clean by washing your hands before and after touching raw meat. Also clean any cutting boards, utensils, dishes, or counter spaces you use to prepare meat.

Separate raw meat, seafood, and eggs from fruits, vegetables, and other foods so that they don't become contaminated with bacteria. You should use a separate cutting board for preparing raw meat as well.

Cook meat at high temperatures in order to kill bacteria. Poultry should be cooked to 165 degrees Fahrenheit (75 degrees Celsius). Cook ground beef, veal, pork, and lamb—as well as egg dishes— to 160°F (70°C). Cook fresh pork and whole beef, veal, and lamb to 145°F (65°C). A meat thermometer can be used to check the temperature as you cook.

Chill meats and cooked foods in the refrigerator to prevent the growth and spread of bacteria. Foods in the fridge should be kept lower than 40°F (4°C), and foods should be put in the refrigerator within 2 hours of cooking them, or sooner if it's a hot day.

You can influence food production through the types of food your family eats. To start, you can eat produce that's in season. Just be sure to wash all fruits and vegetables, and peel them if necessary. Cook meat thoroughly and understand food safety. Learn where your food comes from, and if you can, ask the producer how it was made. Be informed about how foods

It's important to chill foods in the refrigerator after cooking. If the temperature is over 90°F (32°C), food should be refrigerated within 1 hour.

are labeled and know which labels to look for based on your food values.

If you feel strongly about the dangers of antibiotics, pesticides, and hormones, you and your family can choose to avoid foods made with these substances when possible. What you buy sends a powerful message to food producers.

All fruits and vegetables should be washed under running water before you eat them.

In addition, you can encourage the government to protect people, animals, and the environment with regulations and bans on dangerous substances. This can be done by writing letters to leaders about these issues and by voting for leaders who share your values about food safety. Until you're old enough to vote, you can encourage older family members to consider these issues when voting.

Food for Thought

1. What prevents people from eating organic food?
2. Now that you know more about antibiotics, pesticides, and hormones, are there things you want to change about the way you eat?
3. What can you do to affect the use of antibiotics, pesticides, and hormones in the food industry?

Alzheimer's disease: A disease that gets worse over time and causes people to lose memory and mental functions.

attention-deficit/hyperactivity disorder: A complex mental health condition that causes people to struggle with impulse control, focusing, and organization.

biomagnification: The process whereby a substance increases in concentration the higher it moves up the food chain.

cast: The nitrogen- and phosphate-containing waste product of earthworms.

contaminate: To make something impure or infected.

genetically engineered: Refers to an organism whose DNA has been changed in a laboratory.

immune system: The system that protects your body from diseases and infections.

nervous system: The body's command center that operates from the brain.

Parkinson's disease: A progressive disease of the nervous system that causes muscular tension and tremors.

puberty: A time of intense hormonal activity during a child's development.

residue: A substance that remains behind.

resistance: The natural ability of an organism to survive or avoid a substance that is toxic to it.

sterility: The inability to reproduce.

synthetic: Something produced artificially.

Books

Allman, Toney. *How Antibiotics Changed the World*. San Diego, CA: ReferencePoint Press, Inc., 2019.

Bard, Jonathan, and Mariel Bard. *Oops! It's Penicillin!* New York, NY: Gareth Stevens, 2020.

Hansen, Grace. *Help the Honeybees*. Minneapolis, MN: Abdo Kids Jumbo, 2019.

Websites

EWG's Shopper's Guide to Pesticides in Produce
www.ewg.org/foodnews/summary.php
This guide comes out every year with reviews of fruits and vegetables with the most and least pesticides.

Food and Drug Administration
www.fda.gov/food
The FDA regularly updates their website with information about food recalls, food safety, healthy diet recommendations, and nutrition facts.

Seafood Watch
www.seafoodwatch.org/
This free online resource ranks seafood safety and sustainability based on type, location, and how it was raised.

Organizations

Environmental Working Group (EWG)
1250 I Street NW, Suite 1000
Washington, DC 20005
www.ewg.org/
The EWG is committed to educating people about the harmful
substances in their food and campaigning to remove toxins from
products and the environment.

National Resources Defense Council (NRDC)
40 West 20th Street, 11th Floor
New York, NY 10011
www.nrdc.org
The NRDC is an organization devoted to protecting the
environment. They focus on food and agricultural practices
that could be harmful, and they provide suggestions for staying
healthy and aware.

World Health Organization
WHO Headquarters, Avenue Appia 20, 1211
Geneva 27, Switzerland
www.who.int/
The World Health Organization provides guidance for people
around the world on how to eat healthy foods and avoid
substances that harm health.

Publisher's note to educators and parents: Our editors have carefully reviewed these websites
to ensure that they are suitable for students. Many websites change frequently, however, and we
cannot guarantee that a site's future contents will continue to meet our high standards of quality and
educational value. Be advised that students should be closely supervised whenever they access
the internet.

I

integrated pest management
(IPM), 37

L

labels, 5, 15, 35–36, 39

M

mastitis, 14
meat, 4, 9, 12–13, 18–19, 27,
34–35, 37–39
medicine, 9, 17
milk, 12–15, 18, 21, 28

N

neonicotinoids, 29

O

organic, 5, 27, 32–35, 37, 41

P

peeling, 18, 33
pests, 4, 10, 31, 35, 37
pigs, 12
pollinators, 26–27, 29–31
population, 7, 29, 37
poultry, 12, 38
pregnancy, 23
proteins, 4, 6, 11

R

recombinant bovine growth
hormone (rBGH), 12–15, 36

S

Salmonella, 18, 21
soil, 10, 27, 30–31, 37
steroids, 11–12

U

U.S. Department of Agriculture
(USDA), 4–5, 24, 32, 35

V

vegetables, 4–6, 9, 16, 30,
33–34, 37–38, 40
veterinarian, 9

W

washing, 16, 18, 20, 33, 38
water, 9–10, 12, 18, 21, 24,
27, 29, 30, 37, 40
World Health Organization
(WHO), 24

About the Author

Rachael Morlock is a freelance writer and copyeditor. She is the author of several nonfiction and picture books for children and enjoys researching new subjects through her work. In the past, she worked as the coordinator of a Community Supported Bakery. Rachael is always interested in supporting local farmers and food producers in Western New York, where she lives with her dog, Rilke.